Dream Catcher

A YOUNG PERSON'S JOURNAL FOR EXPLORING DREAMS

PATRICIA GARFIELD, Ph.D.

TUNDRA BOOKS

Published in Canada by Tundra Books,
481 University Avenue, Toronto, Ontario M5G 2E9

Published in the United States by Tundra Books of Northern New York,
P.O. Box 1030, Plattsburgh, New York 12901

Library of Congress Control Number: 2003102657

National Library of Canada Cataloguing in Publication

Garfield, Patricia L.
Dream catcher : a young person's journal for exploring dreams / Patricia Garfield.

ISBN 0-88776-661-7

1. Dreams–Juvenile literature. I. Title.

BF1099.C55G373 2003   j154.6'3   C2003-901083-X

We acknowledge the financial support of the Government of Canada through the
Book Publishing Industry Development Program (BPIDP) and that of the
Government of Ontario through the Ontario Media Development Corporation's
Ontario Book Initiative. We further acknowledge the support of the Canada Council
for the Arts and the Ontario Arts Council for our publishing program.

Design: Cindy Reichle

Printed and bound in Canada

1 2 3 4 5 6   08 07 06 05 04 03

Setting Your Stage
for Sweet Dreams

When you climb into bed tonight, take a good look around you. Before you turn the light out, what do you see? What objects do you have where you sleep? Are there posters on the walls?

What do you have near your head? Perhaps you've set a glass of water, an alarm clock, a bedside lamp, or a box of tissues on your bedside stand. Maybe there's a special photograph. You might even have a notepad and pen so you can jot down your dreams.

Do you own stuffed animals, favorite dolls or action figures? Many kids keep these for bed decorations long after they've stopped playing with them. Kids of all ages have favorite pillows and blankets, sometimes finding it hard to sleep without their special objects. Or you might tuck a certain something under your pillow – a memento from a concert, a photo of a sweetheart or a wished-for love.

Whatever it is that you keep near your head, under your pillow, or within your range of sight – whatever you gaze at or hold as you grow sleepy – is certain to influence your dreams during the night. People are very suggestible during the drowsy time before sleep, so what you find yourself thinking about then is important. Prayers or thoughts and worries – things inside your head – are most powerful at this time.

When you put decorations and mementos in your sleeping place, you are echoing an ancient practice for safe sleep and good dreams. You might be amazed to discover how people throughout history have tried

to protect themselves during sleep while coaxing happy dreams. Some of these techniques are surprisingly effective. You may want to try a few of them as you explore your dream territory with *Dream Catcher* as your "map."

But this book is not just about dreams; it's about *your* dreams. It's a journal, so you'll want to set it and a pen near your bed, ready to use after you've caught a dream. Some kids like to record their dreams in their journal as soon as they have them, straight from the pillow. Other kids prefer to make rough notes on a notepad and later transfer these to their journal in clearer handwriting. Any way that works for you is fine. Look at the beginning of the Dream Catcher Journal section for tips on keeping your journal and working with your dreams.

In memory of my mother, Evelyn, whose fascination with dreams inspired me to start a dream journal when I was fourteen, little realizing she'd launched a career.

Keeping a Dream Journal

Your dreams are like a window that opens into a storeroom of hidden thoughts and secret feelings. That flash of anger you controlled in the daytime, those tears of hurt you stifled so no one saw, your worry about things that might happen, your joy at a success, your hope for a bright future – all these emotions and others are acted out each night on the stage of your dreams.

Keeping a dream journal will show clearly what's been playing at your inner dream theater. It will help bring fabulous coming attractions with happy endings, whether you're asleep or awake. Your dreams help shape your life.

★ Safe Sleep and Bright Dreams ★

The idea that people are vulnerable during sleep has been around for thousands of years. People in ancient times believed that the soul could travel while the body was asleep, leaving the body in danger of attack by demons during the dark night. Today, people have not totally lost that age-old inborn fear of the dark.

When Megan was little, her parents took her to a party of adults and put her to sleep in a spare bedroom where the coats of the guests were piled. Her mother left the door ajar, so only a little light filtered into the room. The girl could hear the murmur of the adults talking in the living room. At first she felt comfortable, but as her eyes adjusted to the dark, strange shapes emerged. She saw someone or something lurking behind the half-open door – monster-like with a bulky body and outstretched arms. Was it coming closer?

Too terrified to stir, Megan began to sob and then to wail. Soon heavy footsteps sounded on the stairs. The door was thrown open and the overhead light switched on. Then Megan could clearly see that the "monster" behind the door was a man's bathrobe, its sleeves dangling. She felt immense relief, but also felt embarrassed and childish to have made such a fuss.

Even though you're much older, you too may sometimes feel uneasy lying in bed in the dark, watching moving shadows or listening to odd creaks and other night sounds. Instead of climbing into bed, some kids leap in to avoid any danger lurking beneath it. Sleepers have always needed safeguards. For protection, folk through the ages in many lands would hang a "charm" near the sleeping person.

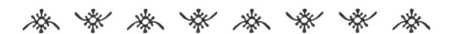

These old-time practices may give you some useful ideas to feel safer as you sleep.

☆ *Your Enchanted Bedroom* ☆

The stuffed animals, small dolls, or action figures that you keep in your bedroom are a modern form of helpful elves and fairies, descendants of ancient gods and goddesses, who were once believed to ensure safe sleep and happy dreams.

Almost all kids have something they want near them as they sleep. Lindsay has a collection of seventy stuffed animals lined along the bedside wall. From these, she chooses a different one each night to cuddle as she drifts to sleep, feeling safe under its protection. Megan loves to curl around a soft green felt frog her godmother made. Jake has a quilt his grandmother made from silk patches; he likes to feel the smooth material as he goes to sleep. Mady holds an old silk nightgown of her mother's against her cheek.

In a real sense, the decorations in your bedroom can help you feel secure and have happy dreams. When Alexandra gazes at her poster of running horses, she remembers the happy sensation she has when riding. Sherry keeps a huge print of Justin Timberlake on her bedroom wall. Matt has pictures from Star Wars.

You'll want to choose carefully whose portraits you hang on your wall, have beside your bed or under your pillow. They are like the icons in ancient temples and on home altars. If you have photographs of people close to you, their pictures keep you connected to the love

they hold for you. If the pictures are of movie, television, or music stars, they call to mind the qualities these people represent for you – you probably want to develop these aspects of yourself.

You can create a safe haven in your bedroom by the objects and images you choose to place around you.

☆ *A Place to Rest Your Head* ☆

Everyone knows that a soft fluffy pillow, filled with feathers or foam, is what you put under your head to sleep, right? But people in some cultures did not use pillows like the ones you are familiar with, which may have been too hot for comfort in warm climates. In ancient Egypt, all sleepers used hard objects that, although they were called headrests, actually supported the neck during sleep. The poor slept on simple ones that looked like a small table with a slightly curved top. Rich people slept on elaborate ones decorated with safeguarding figures.

Many Asian cultures thought that soft pillows "rob vitality" from the body. They, too, had wooden headrests. Wealthy people would sleep resting on porcelain neck supports decorated with lucky designs. One popular headrest was in the form of a crouching boy holding a kind of mushroom thought to ensure long life, as it was meant to guarantee the birth of a son as well as longevity for the sleeper.

Even today, some Asians choose hard headrests. A Chinese woman in New York says she sleeps on a "jade pillow," a rectangle of solid

jade carved with a slight indentation to accommodate the head. She says the stone is cool and buttery, and sleeping on it feels as if she's been "massaged for eight hours." In her tradition, jade is a magical substance certain to bring good fortune.

☆ *Night Music* ☆

Many kids listen to music while falling asleep. Peter loves to hear classical music playing when he's drowsy. Nick listens to the softer songs of his favorite bands through headphones as he drifts off to sleep.

Kids who are musically talented may hear original music in their dreams. The singer Tori Amos, for instance, is said to compose many of her complex songs based on her dreams.

Aboriginal North Americans traditionally went on vision quests when they reached puberty. A young person on a quest often dreamed of meeting a spirit guide, who disclosed the dreamer's role in life (medicine man, warrior, midwife) and taught them a "power song." For the remainder of the person's life, this tune was sung softly to call on the spirit guide's strength. The treasured melodies were kept secret or shared only with family members, usually prior to death.

Music heard in a dream has great emotional power for the dreamer. If your dreams reverberate with melody, try to remember the tune. You may have caught hold of your own inner power song.

✫ *The Powers in Dream Charms Live Today* ✫

When you surround yourself with your favorite things as you sleep, you are using them as personal charms. Charms from times past can be useful to today's dreamers. Their powers are still alive. There may or may not be evil spirits that attack you while you sleep, but there surely are nightmares. There may or may not be magic, but there are objects that make people feel secure and help them to have inspiring dreams.

Do you want to be more relaxed? Do you wish for great adventures? Want to visit beautiful places and witness amazing things? Talk with miraculous animals? See loved people who have died? Get help when you feel frightened? Feel safer and stronger? Connect with someone or something inspiring? All these experiences can be found in your dreams. The pictures in your dreams are powers that already live within you. If you learn to recognize them, you can make them part of your waking world.

In your dreams, you can seek and find the unique images that empower you. They are waiting for you to discover them and bring them to life.

★ Catching Your Dreams ★

You'll need some of your own dreams before you can launch a quest of inner discovery. In addition to the traditions for catching dreams that

you'll find in the part of this book called Dream Catchers from Around the World, there are certain basic steps that will help.

- You need to get a reasonable amount of sleep. Although most young people have many more dreams than they can manage because of the upsurge of hormones at adolescence, they often don't get enough regular sleep. Just keep in mind that the more you sleep, the more you dream. You'll dream about 20 percent of the time you're asleep. Dreams are distributed throughout the night in increasingly long segments. The first dream of the night is only about ten minutes in length. The dream most people remember is the last one toward morning. If you've slept eight hours, it will last a half-hour or more.

- With a hectic school schedule you might not have time to write down your dreams before getting the day underway. A good time to go fishing for dreams is on a weekend, holiday, or vacation when you can sleep in. When you awaken naturally (not by alarm clock, radio, or someone calling you) you'll be waking up from a dream.

- Lie still for a few minutes with your eyes shut. Notice what's going through your mind. Even if they are not part of a dream, morning thoughts are often connected to the dream that preceded them. If you don't recall anything in the position you were in when you woke up, roll gently to another sleep position you use. People often find it easier to remember dreams when they are in the same body position as the one when they had the dream.

- Pay attention to any lingering picture or phrase in your mind. Jot down a few words on the notepad you've placed by your bed. Later,

when you're up and have time, you can transfer the rough notes into your Dream Catcher Journal.

Sometimes it's all too easy to recall a dream. You might be startled awake in the middle of the night by a dreadful nightmare. It's simpler to remember scary dreams because they are so intense. Since they often wake you up, their images are very fresh. Write down the key parts of any dream that shocks you out of sleep. Such dreams are important to understand, because they're connected to significant feelings about current events in your life.

On the other hand, you might awaken feeling the pleasure of soaring across the sky, surveying the world below. Maybe you're hitting the winning run in a baseball game. Or perhaps the love of your life is embracing you. These good dreams are meaningful, too. Make a note of your dream delights as well as the terrors.

★ Understanding Your Dreams ★

Okay, you've caught some dreams. Now what? What do you do with them? How do you make sense of the weird and wild pictures that lit up last night's dream?

★ *Dream Pictures are Feeling Pictures* ★

The first thing you need to know is that dream images are pictures of your emotions. They tell you how you feel about some waking issue at

a particular moment in time. Your dream life is like a movie of your emotional life. Each dream image tells you something significant about how you really feel right now.

Feeling shaky in your relationship with your sweetie? You might dream about an earthquake rattling the ground under your feet, or about that person cuddling with another. Breaking up a relationship? You might dream about buildings coming apart and collapsing, or of volcanoes erupting. Hurting from cruel words a classmate flung at you? You might have a nightmare about being attacked by sharks with sharp teeth.

Dreams don't just depict the bad stuff. Are you feeling good about your current looks? In tonight's dream you might be wearing the coolest outfit imaginable. Noticed a new girl or guy in class who interests you? You might be nuzzling an adorable puppy or some other playful young animal in a dream tonight. Getting good at a sport you've been practicing? You might dream of driving a fabulous car with skill and ease through tricky terrain.

Your dreams are a kind of picture language made up from your feelings. Like any language you don't speak fluently, you need to learn some basic vocabulary. With this knowledge you'll become more fluent with "dreamish" every night.

✮ *Rerun Dreams* ✮

Anytime you have a repetitive dream it's vital to understand it. A recurring dream suggests a recurring situation or problem that's unresolved.

If you have a repetitive dream, mark it with a star in your Dream Catcher Journal. Take a few minutes to describe or define the key images in it and record them. Also make note of what happened during the day before the dream recurs. You'll often find a clue to what set off that same old dream again.

Roberto frequently dreams that he's in the back seat of a moving car with no driver. His recurrent dream shouts, "I have no control over my life!" Roberto surely has the impression that he can't steer his way through his waking life. Things are out of his power to control and no one's in charge. Perhaps his family doesn't seem to care about him, or maybe they are absent. Roberto feels alone in a situation that could lead to a collision. Recurrent dreams like his are warnings to pay attention and get help before there's an emotional crash.

☆ *Special Occasion Dreams* ☆

You may find yourself having special dreams at certain times during the year. Many people do. Your birthday eve, for instance, can bring on a unique dream about your fears, hopes, or wishes for the age you've reached. On his birthday eve, Tom dreamed of falling into a muddy hole, expressing some murky concern. Cindy dreamed of playing in a garden with a beautiful unicorn the night before her birthday, suggesting she felt optimistic about her future.

You might have a fabulous dream about a forthcoming vacation or school holiday, anticipating good times. Raj dreamed of happily riding

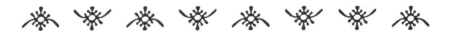

the train with his family to visit his favorite aunt just before holiday time, forecasting his hope for good times ahead.

If you had an accident, or someone you loved died at a certain time of year, you might have an "anniversary dream" at the same time the following year, expressing sadness or feeling a distinct connection. On the anniversary of his grandmother's death, Billy dreamed she sat beside him on the bed and stroked his hair while telling him she'd always love him. Billy was comforted by this dream.

★ Basic Dream Themes ★

From time to time your dreams are sure to depict fear, frustration, love, and fun. There are oodles of variations on these four basic areas, but here's a skeletal version. (You can read in more detail about different dream themes in *The Dream Book: A Young Person's Guide to Understanding Dreams.*)

✷ *Fearful Dreams* ✷

The most common nightmare for people of all ages in every country is being chased or attacked by some person, animal, thing, or dark presence. The attacker varies from country to country, but the scenario is the same. You see the horrid thing. It pursues you. You run and try to escape or hide. It closes in on you and, just as it's about to grab you, you awake in terror. What a relief to find it's "only a dream!"

Other alarming dream themes include being wounded or killed, falling, drowning, being caught in a natural disaster such as a tidal wave or fire, being in a war zone, or being threatened by someone who is dead.

No matter how gruesome that nightmare you just had might be, it contains something you need to know and something you need to do.

For instance, take Anne's dream:

I am in my parents' bathroom with my mom and a female lion. I am preparing to leave when the lioness blocks my way. My mother reads a newspaper in the corner next to the mirrors and seems to be disinterested. I try to escape by dodging around a large central counter (not really there) but to no avail. Each time I turn to rethink my strategy in the corner closer to my mom, the lioness sinks her claws into my Achilles tendons and drags me back. The lioness' eyes are green.

Anne woke up with anxiety from this dream. It contains elements of both fear and frustration. She wants to do something but is prevented by someone or something that frightens her.

Anne says that her parents' bathroom is significant because she has spent lots of time over the years talking to her reflection in the mirrors there. She is saying something revealing to herself in this dream.

To explore her dream, Anne writes it down as she recalls it during the night on a notepad, or the next morning in her dream journal. Whenever you record a dream, it's important to *write it in the present*

tense. This helps you get in touch with the emotion of the dream, gives you better recall, and starts to defuse any discomfort.

Anne's not sure who or what the lioness stands for in her nightmare. She needs to ask herself questions about it. Whenever you dream about an animal you can understand its meaning better by doing a little dream detective work.

In Anne's case, she needs to ask herself these questions:

- Who do I know who has green eyes? (Identifying a main quality of attacker's appearance.)
- What are green-eyed people like? Are they jealous of someone?
- How would I describe a lioness to a little kid who never saw or heard of one? How is a lioness different from other wild animals with four legs? (Description of attacker, how it differs from similar ones, and any experiences you've had with something like it.)
- Who or what is blocking my way from where I want to go or what I want to do during the daytime? (Associations with similar feelings while awake.)
- Who or what is digging sharply into my weak spots in waking life? (Associations with similar waking-life experience.)

When you have a bad dream, you want to examine the appearance and action of the characters in your dream and the setting in which it takes place. Adjust the questions above to fit your dream, ask them of yourself, and jot down your responses in your dream journal near the description of the dream. Remember that dreams exaggerate, so your dreams about waking-life happenings will be more dramatic than the actual event.

☆ *The Setting of Your Dream* ☆

In Anne's dream she knows that her parents' bathroom is a place where she not only checks out her appearance in the many mirrors but also reflects on her inner thoughts.

Your dream might take place in a dangerous area of an inner city, or on the edge of a cliff, or in the basement of your house, or on a muddy road in a rainstorm, or in a brightly lit ballroom with polished floors. Wherever you set your dream tells you about your emotional mood at the time. Anne was in a fairly normal reflective place. It was altered by the presence of an island-type counter that would be more usual in a kitchen – a place where her mother would be likely to be preparing nourishment.

☆ *The Action in Your Dream* ☆

In Anne's dream there are three characters: her mother, herself, and the lioness. The lioness is blocking Anne and attacking her weak spots (her ankles, the only spot where the Greek hero Achilles was vulnerable and so received his fatal wound) while her mother ignores the whole thing. The key words are "blocking," "attacking," and "ignoring."

Always try to grasp the overall gist of your dream first. Since we know that dreams tell us about our emotional response to events in waking life, we know that Anne feels blocked from something she

wants to do, or somewhere she wants to go. She feels attacked in her vulnerable spots and ignored by the person who should be helping her.

☆ *Dialogue with Your Dream* ☆

The precise meaning of Anne's dream will depend on her answers to the questions she asks herself. Suppose Anne replied to the first question, "Actually, my eyes are green. I always hate it when people talk about the green-eyed monster of jealousy." This reply would link Anne herself to the attacking lion. It would suggest that she feels deeply angry, as mad as a ferocious lion, perhaps jealous of someone, and is not able to escape this feeling no matter how she dodges it.

Suppose Anne had answered the first question by saying, "My mother has the most beautiful clear, green eyes. They're so unusual. Everyone admires them." Now the meaning of her dream shifts because the dreamer's answer links the lion's green eyes to her mother. Does Anne feel that some fierce part of her mom prevents her from developing in a way she desires? Does the dreamer feel resentful of her mother? The mother in Anne's dream could represent her actual mom who's not doing her job of protecting her daughter, or it could be the mom-part of Anne who should be doing a better job of protecting herself.

If Anne had said, "I don't know anyone who has green eyes. I always thought they meant envy," her green-eyed lioness would refer to the emotion of envy in herself or her mother.

Another revealing technique in dream work is to let the image speak for itself, give it a voice in your imagination. For example, Anne's lion might say, *You say you want to understand yourself but you never pay any attention to me. I have to trap you and claw your ankles to get you to notice me. I'm the lion inside you. I'm angry. I'm powerful. You need my lion-energy. You need to learn to stand up for yourself. I won't hurt you; I'll help you if you listen. Look into my eyes and feel my strength.*

Anne's dream teaches her something about the lioness part of herself, or of her mom, or of some other female in her waking life. It also tells her she needs to do something about this fact, depending on what she's learned. For instance, Anne might need to learn to speak up for herself, to let her lion-strength become more active.

> When you dream of a character you wonder about, always consider these things:
> - Who or what does this dream animal or person remind me of?
> - What are the main traits of this dream animal or person?
> - How does this dream animal or person differ from other similar ones?

All this may sound very complicated if you haven't worked with your dreams before. It's rather like working a jigsaw puzzle. At first the pieces don't seem to fit, but suddenly you grasp the whole picture and everything begins to fall into place. Just start by recording your dreams, asking yourself questions about them, and noting your answers. Soon you'll start to understand your personal dream language.

★ *Frustration Dreams* ★

Have you ever dreamed about missing a bus? You're almost at the door when it pulls away without you. You've probably dreamed about being naked in public, as Jack did when he dreamed about being at school and everyone laughing because he had no pants on. Suppose you dream about driving a car when suddenly the brakes don't work? Or maybe you are one of the many people who dream about being in a classroom, ready to take a test, when you find that the questions are on a different subject entirely, one you've never studied.

Perhaps you've had the maddening dream about being lost in a maze or in hallways, unable to find the exit. You might be partially paralyzed in a dream, struggling hard to move your legs that feel as if they are heavy as lead. Have you ever dreamed about trying to use a telephone but can't get it to function properly? You could dream of missing some valued possession, as Connie did when she dreamed that, ten minutes before she was to go onstage, she lost a bright blue wig she needed for a karaoke performance.

These dream themes – and many variations on them – express our feelings about the obstacles we confront. Our lives have numerous frustrations as well as anxieties. Strange as it may seem, dealing with them in your dreams will help you surmount the hurdles in your waking hours.

Martin often has this dream:

I'm lost in a strange landscape, usually mountains or tunnels. Sometimes it's inside films or video games.

You need to question yourself about the images in your repetitive dream. In Martin's case he could ask himself these questions:

- What is a mountain? What makes it different from other high places? (Define or describe key image in dream.)
- What is a tunnel? How is it different from other enclosed places? (Define or describe another key image in dream.)
- Why would being lost in the mountains or in tunnels be worse than elsewhere? (Differentiate between key images and other similar ones.)

Like most people, Martin would probably say that mountain terrain is difficult and sometimes treacherous. He might say that tunnels often go under mountains, but can be risky places because of potential collapse or entrapment. Being lost in either place could be life-threatening. If these were his answers, Martin's dreams would express an ongoing problem in waking life that feels difficult and tricky to get across or through.

On the other hand, if Martin was a professional mountain climber, the same dream might suggest discontent with his chosen career.

What about getting lost inside a movie or video game? Again, we need Martin's descriptions of these objects to be sure of the meaning for him. He might well say that these entertainment items are very complex, and he has trouble figuring out how to win. These replies would help Martin grasp the connection between his recurrent dream and the struggle to cope with his waking-life situation.

In frustration dreams, as well as in fearful ones, dreamers have far more control than they realize. You'll see that there is much you can do to improve any nightmare.

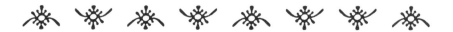

✫ *Dreams of Love* ✫

Romantic dreams are among the favorite dreams for people of any age. Lots of kids dream about being in love with a famous music, movie, or TV star, as Carolyn did about one of the Backstreet Boys who – in her dream – loved her passionately in return.

Perhaps you dream of dancing in a romantic setting or cuddling with a crush. You might find yourself making out with your favorite hottie in a delicious dream of love. Dream lovers can be totally imaginary or they might be a girl or guy from your geometry class. Maybe you even dream of snuggling with someone you find repellent in waking life.

Many kids have delightful dreams about hugging and kissing their current boyfriends or girlfriends. But these dreams can become worrisome if they involve the waking-life lover being intimate with someone else. Or dreamers themselves snuggle with a different lover and wake up feeling profoundly guilty. They're puzzled and want to know what's going on. Such dreams often reflect insecurity in the relationship or low self-confidence.

The crucial thing to realize in dreams about love is that, when you caress a person in a dream, it does not necessarily mean you desire that actual person. You'll know if that person himself or herself is truly attractive to you. More often the real attraction is some quality the person has that you – the dreamer – desire for yourself.

Here are some tips for detecting the meaning of your dream love:

- Who is the lover in your dream? Write a short sentence describing the kind of person he or she is.
- List three outstanding attributes of this person. What's special?
- Could you use any of these attributes in yourself at the present time?
- Does the dream lover's name have a symbolic meaning?
- Do the dream lover's name or looks resemble someone you know?

Think about your responses to these questions and jot down the descriptions in your journal.

Daniel dreamed about kissing the movie actor Kirsten Dunst. He described her as "sweet, sensitive, vulnerable." Since Daniel is into sports, including weightlifting, his dream may have been a reminder to stay in touch with a sensitive side of himself, to not lose touch with it, as well as picturing a type of woman who appealed to him.

Monica kept having romantic dreams about a former boyfriend named Art. She had absolutely no further interest in being that particular boy's girlfriend, so her dreams confused her. Thinking about the possibility of a pun on his name, Monica realized that she had neglected her painting, something she used to do that gave her much pleasure. Her dreams were reminding her of the value of *art* and to reconnect with that quality in her life.

Kaitlin had recurrent romantic dreams about a strange man dressed all in green. Her associations to the color green were with

Ireland, the country of her heritage. On one level, Kaitlin was yearning for an Irish boyfriend. Strangely, not only did she eventually marry an Irish man, but his last name was Green. Sometimes dreams seem stranger than fiction.

Dream lovers and famous people in your dreams may represent connections with power, artistic sensitivity, grace, emotion, spirituality, or some other characteristic. If you dream about relating romantically to someone you dislike, your dream may be a warning that you're hooking up with something bad for you.

By paying attention to dreams about a celebrity, whether that person shows up as a lover or simply as a presence in your dream, you will help balance your waking life. Such dreams are reminders of what is significant to you right now, and what you feel you need to be a more complete person. Exploring your dreams at this level leads to self-discovery and prepares for waking adventures.

☆ *Fun Dreams* ☆

You've probably already found that dreams can bring happy times. Aside from enchanting dreams of dance or romance, flying dreams head the all-star list.

Jin had this dream:

I see flying trains in a magical kingdom. I read a book by an author named Hunter and am transported to this magical place.

You, too, might dream of soaring high in the night sky to enchanted places. Ecstatic dreams of flight most often take place when we feel really good about some accomplishment in daily life, or when things in general are flourishing.

You, like many kids, might have exciting dreams of excelling at your favorite sport, playing on a top-class sports team as an equal, or starring in a film or performing on stage to great acclaim. You might be given a precious gift or have a loving visit with someone who died. Perhaps you come up with an amazingly creative idea. You could receive knowledge that feels as if it was sent from another world. You might dream of being in touch with a place beyond space and time, a realm of the spirit. Some dreams inspire and lift dreamers to such an extent that their entire lives are transformed.

These "higher levels" of dreaming are more likely to occur when you have coped with some of the fears and frustrations in typical dreams. Read on for some useful suggestions for befriending your dreams.

★ Changing Your Dreams ★

You have far more resources in your dreams than you realize. Nightmares about being pursued by something horrific are almost certain to occur at some point in your life. Dreamers typically run and try to escape or hide from the villain after them. Many dreamers awake in a panic to get away from the dream danger.

Try staying asleep and facing it instead. All you have to do is *remember that you are in a dream*. It's your dream, imaginatively composed of your emotional reactions to problems in your waking life.

When you manage to stay asleep and confront the dream danger, it almost always transforms into a less threatening form. That dream tiger after you may turn into a kitten. The grotesque witch who wants to tear your throat out may stop in her tracks when you tell her, "You're a dream figure and you can't hurt me!" The shark that's trying to take a chunk out of your side may turn and swim away when you give it a sharp rap on the nose.

And don't forget that you can call in reinforcements. You can have anyone or anything you want enter your dream. Get help! When you are facing overwhelming odds, make them even. Any strong figure can enter your dream when you call on it. When Amy felt at risk in a dream, she would call her family dog to come to her protection. Neil shouted for Mighty Joe Young to come to his aid. Richie yelled for Ultraman, who helped him fend off a lion attack in his nightmare. Suzanne had Superman rescue her from the bridge from which she was about to tumble into deep waters.

In a recurrent dream, recognize it for the same nightmare you've had before. You might realize, "I'm having that same scary dream again! It's a dream. I can change it."

In the middle of a terrifying nightmare about a tidal wave, Daisy found she could breathe underwater. An amazing number of dreamers

have made the same discovery. You can fall gently and land softly instead of bolting awake with alarm. In a dream about poisonous warfare, put on a gas mask and help others. You can reach in your pocket for a weapon, a flashlight, and a map to fight off trouble or find your way out of a maze. Dream allies and dream tools are at your fingertips when you remember that you have the power to change your dreams.

Some kids have been able to "overfeed" the monsters in their dreams, or simply glue their mouths shut, rendering them harmless. Others have made friends with the bad guys in their dreams; still others surround them with golden light to tame and gentle them.

Sound like magic? It has worked for thousands of dreamers – sometimes at the first try, sometimes after several attempts. The really magical part is how taking action within a scary dream changes your waking life. When your dream enemies wound or kill you, you wake up feeling shaky much of the following day. Things can go from bad to worse. You may even become reluctant to go to sleep. However, when you confront your dream enemies, ward off danger, and succeed in defeating the bad guys or befriending them, you wake up feeling good. Your self-confidence soars. You are more able to deal with the waking-life problems the nightmares represent. You feel good and your waking life gets better.

Your dream life improves, too. Because you know you can cope with distressing situations, you are free to enjoy dream adventures. You start a positive cycle in which your dreams support your waking hours, which in turn enrich your future dreaming.

- When in dream danger, don't run, hide, or wake up.
- Get help, but struggle by yourself until help comes.
- Remember that it's *your* dream.
- You have the power to create change for the better in any dream you have.
- For recurrent nightmares, imagine a better, improved ending, then recall your intention the next time the bad dream occurs.

✰ *Changing Your Life* ✰

As you learn the skill of changing your dreams, nightmares will decrease. You'll find that taking action makes a difference in waking life as well as in dreams. You'll discover that you have more power than you ever dreamed possible. Asleep or awake, you'll be creating a newer and stronger self, open to the wonders of the whole of life.

Dream Catchers from Around the World

You've probably heard about dream catchers used by different First Nations peoples of North America. The original ones were made from a willow branch shaped into a hoop and filled with a web made of sinew. They were decorated with feathers and beads.

If you had been a child of one of these Nations, your mother would probably have made a dream catcher for you and suspended it from the top of your cradleboard by a cord made of plum bark stained red with bloodroot. Swaddled in the cradleboard, you could watch the feather decorations dangling from the dream catcher while you were awake. When you fell asleep, your mother could be sure of your steady breathing by the soft movement of the feathers.

Adults, too, often hung dream catchers above their sleeping spaces. In the same way that a spider's web catches flies, it was believed that the webbing of the dream catcher filtered out nightmares that were at large during darkness. When the sun rose at dawn, these trapped bad dreams would evaporate, just as the morning dew dried up on a spider's web.

Dream catchers usually had a few pretty stones, crystals, or beads woven into the web. These were thought to attract good dreams, which passed through the center opening to enter the sleeper's mind with their beautiful images, songs of power, and healing cures.

★ Finding Your Own Dream Catcher ★

These days, many people like to hang dream catchers or replicas of them near where they sleep. Whether you have an actual dream catcher or simply imagine one, it can remind you of your ability to sift through your dreams. It recalls your capacity to defend yourself against what is too difficult to think about at the moment, even in a dream. It can help you embrace what you feel ready for and open to cope with at the present time. Dream catchers are reminders that great dreams have the power to change our lives. Catch your dreams and begin to discover your innermost self. *Dream Catcher* can get you started on an exciting journey.

Here, you'll find examples of other types of dream catchers used in different cultures throughout time. These variations on the dream catcher emphasize different special qualities that could be appealing to you. If you feel a connection with any of these dream catchers, you might make your own for your bedside, or you could invent your own version. The main thing is to catch your dreams. Then you can start unlocking the power that's inside them, waiting for you to claim it as your own.

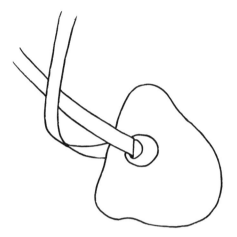

⭐ *The Dream Stone* ⭐

If you had been born in prehistoric times, your parents might have provided you with a dream stone to make you feel safe during the night. First they would search for a stone with a natural hole gradually formed by the action of water. Through the hole, rolled bark or reed would be strung. From the juice of berries or bloodroot, the reed would have been dyed red, a color believed to repel evil spirits since it is the color of life, of blood.

Imagine yourself in a cave at night, curled facing the fire in the center of your family. Above you on the rock wall or clutched in your hand is your dream stone. Its hard surface reminds you to be as strong as a rock against evil spirits and nightmares. Yet the hole allows good dreams to filter through your slumber.

★ *Bes the Egyptian Dwarf God* ★

In ancient Egypt, many people honored Bes. This odd-looking dwarf
god, wearing a lion skin and sticking out his tongue, was especially
powerful in defending children and women. At times he was shown
holding a musical instrument because he was also a god of dance,
drink, and partying. A small image of Bes would be placed at the head
of your bed or, if your family was rich, his shape carved into the head-
board. The pharaoh himself had a folding headrest that was carved
with Bes' face on each side. As Bes guarded the pharaoh's sleep in both
directions, so would he help you recall your own inner strength to
guard yourself and to defend the helpless with the vigor of a lion. He
would remind you that at times your dreams resound with joyful
music and dance.

✮ *The Sacred Mountains Headrest* ✮

In ancient Egypt, sacred picture writing – using hieroglyphics – was used. The hieroglyph for "horizon" was a protective image, showing two mountains with the curve of the sun setting or rising between them. Sometimes instead of mountains, two lions – known as the lions of yesterday and tomorrow – were carved facing opposite directions. If you had a headrest based on this hieroglyph, you could sleep with the mountain shapes on either side of your head protecting you from danger during the night. Your head would take the place of the sun. When you went to sleep, the "sun" would be setting; when you got up in the morning, the "sun" would be rising.

Picture yourself sleeping between sheltering mountains or between the forceful lions of yesterday and tomorrow. You might remember your own capacity for self-protection and your ability to shelter what is precious – your dreams.

★ *The Mirror of Isis* ★

Isis was a powerful goddess and protector of children. Myths tell of
how the evil Seth cut Isis' husband Osiris into pieces that he scattered
around the land of Egypt. Isis found and gathered all the pieces,
magically restoring Osiris to life. If you lived in Mediterranean lands
during the three thousand years that Isis was beloved, you would go
to one of her temples to sleep and dream. You would take a gift of
two mirrors, insuring your lifetime happiness. Sleeping in Isis' temple
of dreams, you would see that, even when your life has been torn into
pieces, you can gather the scattered parts and build a new life. You
would understand the importance of protecting and nourishing
not only the weak, but also your symbolic child – your inner life.
Reflections of the goddess' wisdom would show your dreams as
radiant mirrors, offering you insight every night.

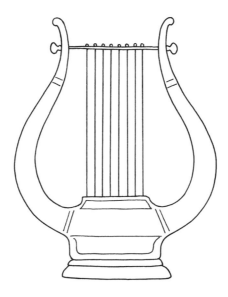

✯ *Orpheus' Lyre* ✯

If you were a child born in ancient Greece, you would know legends of
the singer Orpheus. His poetry, sung to music played on his lyre, or
harp, was so splendid it was capable of soothing savage beasts or even
a storm, and it could dazzle the minds of men. Orpheus was even able
to charm the god of the underworld, Pluto, when he went there to
retrieve his beloved wife Eurydice. He was commanded not to look
back at his wife's spirit until they reached the upper world, but
he could not resist a glance, and so lost her forever. Orpheus' story
reminds you that, although you can never bring back people you love
who have died, you can have comforting and uplifting dreams about
them, listen to their advice, and feel their love once more.

⭐ *Orpheus' Song* ⭐

The famous singer Orpheus is said to have written many hymns. One is a hymn of praise to the "divinity of dreams." People believed that if they sang or chanted this song, they could evoke dreams of the future.

> *Come, blessed power of dreams divine,*
> *Angel of future, swift wings be thine.*
> *Oracle source to all humankind*
> *Gently whisper into my mind.*
> *Through sleep's silence and dark of night*
> *Let thy power awaken inner sight.*
> *In my next dream, the will of heaven relate,*
> *And kindly tell my future fate.*

You might recite this adaptation of the first verse to yourself as you fall asleep. Orpheus' song says that dreams sometimes give you a glimpse of the future. Reciting or singing it before you sleep might reveal what's coming in your life.

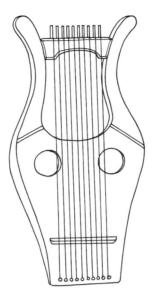

☆ *David's Harp* ☆

David, the shepherd who became the second king of Israel, was said to have slept with a kind of ancient harp, called a kinnor, suspended over his head. This harp didn't need a person to play it, but made music when stroked by the gentle movement of the wind. Perhaps some of King David's songs, the famous psalms he later composed, were evolved from the tender chords he heard during his boyhood dreams. Listen for the music that plays in your dreams – it might be a grand new composition.

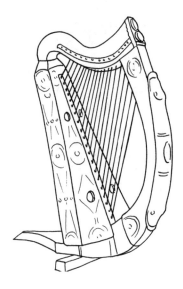

★ *Dagda's Harp* ★

If you lived in Ireland in the time of the Celts, you would hear many tales of the father of the gods, Dagda, and his magical harp. The Celts believed that there were three spellbinding melodies that would enchant the listener. The first was "sleep music" that caused all who heard it to slumber; it was used to immobilize wicked warriors or put the sick to sleep in order to cure them. The second was "laughter music" that could make you giggle, chuckle, and snort uncontrollably until your sides ached. The third was "weeping music," making its listeners wail inconsolably. These beliefs from old Ireland might remind you that the melodies of emotion are playing in your dreams, making you sad or amused, or giving you deep, refreshing rest. The spell that dream music casts is deep.

✯ *The Double-Headed Tiger* ✯

In the China of long ago, you might have a Double-Headed Tiger
pillow. It would look like a stuffed cotton tiger with two large heads
and front paws facing in opposite directions. Your neck would rest on
the body area between the two tiger heads. The tigers' four eyes would
be wide open, watching for danger from any direction. Both foreheads
would be marked with the Chinese character for "number one" because
the tiger was thought to be the most powerful animal. Going to sleep
between the tiger's heads and paws, you would feel its open eyes stand-
ing guard against dream enemies, and watching over you while you
sleep. The Double-Headed Tiger charm can remind you to stay alert
within your dreams, to be aware of danger, while knowing that you
have allies as strong as a tiger. You can freely and safely explore your
adventures in the dreams you catch.

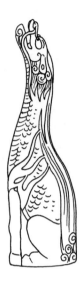

✵ *Baku* ✵

The Japanese mythological creature named Baku had the head and strength of a lion, the scales and might of a dragon, the hooves and fleetness of a horse. Baku ate nightmares. Children were taught that, whenever they had a bad dream, they should call for Baku, saying three times "Devour, O Baku!" The beast would then arrive and gobble up the nightmare as a tasty treat. Sometimes Baku's picture or name would be painted on a child's pillow to remind the dreamer of this mighty ally.

Today Baku can remind you that you have more power in your dreams than you think. By calling for someone strong when facing a dream enemy, you can change a nightmare. You can transform your bad dreams by getting help in dreams while fighting by yourself until help comes. Catching good dreams gets easier when you feel able to cope with nightmares.

✬ *The Treasure Ship* ✬

Many East Asian people believe that what you dream on New Year's Eve foretells your future for the coming year. To help guarantee lucky New Year's dreams, people buy or make a drawing of the lucky gods that are said to sail in on a treasure ship on New Year's Day. The lucky gods bring such gifts as wealth, honesty, beauty, long life, wisdom, dignity, and popularity. If you lived in Japan, you would put a drawing of the treasure ship under your pillow to remind you what fortunate things the year might bring.

At the New Year or on your birthday, you might think about what you would like the coming year to hold. The treasure ship can remind you that sometimes dreams show the path ahead. It can help you remember that what you consider important – wealth, health, strength, beauty, lovingness, wisdom – will shape what you become.

⭐ *The African Dream Doll* ⭐

In South Africa, the Ndebele people practice the art of beading. The tribal healers are women who cure the sick and see the future, skills they learned from ancestors during dreams. To protect sleeping children from evil spirits that cause nightmares, women of the tribe make beaded dolls dressed as healers. These dolls are made of black cotton and decorated with bands of multicolored beads that form a long skirt. Red and white beads form the dolls' eyes. With a Dream Doll set near your sleeping place, the healer's supernatural power to see into the future could come to you in dreams.

The Dream Doll recalls your own power to repel your nightmares. It reminds you that you sometimes get a glimpse of the future in your dreams, and that, when you catch a dream, it can help heal a physical or emotional wound.

⭐ *Johnny Shuteye* ⭐

In Scandinavia there is a unique charm to ensure safe sleep and bright dreams. He's named Johnny Shuteye, a little elf who carries a bag of sand or dust that he sprinkles into the eyes of children to make them sleepy. He also carries a magic umbrella. When he twirls it above the head of a sleeping child, the fantastic pictures on the inside of his umbrella are seen as wondrous dreams by good children. Until recently, children's bedroom lamps were made in the shape of Johnny Shuteye, his umbrella open to form the lampshade. When the light was switched off, the child's dreams were "turned on." Johnny Shuteye can remind you that some dreams are truly fantastic. Picturing his spinning umbrella might help you relax into restful sleep. When you catch a dream of beauty, the light show reveals a clear understanding of your deepest desires.

Dream Catcher Journal

Get ready. The adventure begins here.

    Your dreams are all your own, and so is the way you collect them. Transfer rough notes to this Dream Catcher Journal, or keep it next to your bed and write directly in it without using notes. You might draw sketches and patterns in addition to describing things in words. Maybe you want to group good dreams and bad dreams. Do whatever works best for you.

    Read the boxes with common dreams and their usual meanings to help you start interpreting your dreams.

    Catch a dream and discover yourself.

★ Tips for Keeping a Dream Journal ★

1. Put a notepad and pen within reach before you go to bed.

2. Keep *Dream Catcher* or any other dream journal nearby.

3. In your dream journal, write the date and a short paragraph about any important events and emotions from the daytime. If you are using your Dream Catcher Journal, there are places especially for the Date and Day Notes.

4. Drift off to sleep in whatever way you usually enjoy. When you awaken, in the night or the next morning, scan your mind for dream fragments – key images or phrases – and jot them down on your bedside pad or in your dream journal. The least wisp of a dream can bring back, as you record it, a whole elaborate scenario.

5. Sometime during the day following your dream, transfer your notes to your journal in fuller detail, or fill in the rough notes you've written in your dream journal. Use the present tense in your description. Make a sketch or drawing of any odd images. Mark recurring dreams with a star.

6. Pay attention as you write your dream, noting the villains and dangers, their main characteristics, your heroes and helpers, any animal characters, settings, and the primary action.

7. Notice in particular what protection you had from dream danger. Don't overlook small barriers. The car windshield between you and a villain who tries to attack you literally "shields" you. Your goal is to bring a greater sense of security into your dreams. The safer you feel in dreams, the freer you are to enjoy dream adventures.

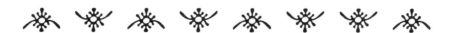

8. Do your emotions change in the course of the dream? Are you feeling terrified and then relieved? Are you feeling normal and then laughing in delight? Shifts in emotion are key moments in a dream and provide clues to its meaning, so notice when they happen.

9. Explore the key images and actions from your dream with some of the techniques like questioning yourself and giving the image a voice.

10. What waking life situation or emotion resembles your dream situation? Note any connections.

11. What's the overall message of your dream? If images in dreams are pictures of your feelings, what is this dream saying to you? Record your best guess in your journal.

12. Are there things you can change today based on your understanding of last night's dream? Bit by bit, dream by dream, you're creating a stronger self.

13. Remember, it's *your* dream. You can change it. You can defuse any fears or frustrations. You can have fun while you discover deeper levels of yourself. Only you can truly understand your dreams because they are formed from your current emotions.

DATE:

DAY NOTES:

Do you dream about being embraced or loved?

You experience or desire waking-life affection. You want to
connect with some quality of the dream lover.

DREAM NOTES:

DATE:

DAY NOTES:

Do you dream about being chased or attacked?

You feel threatened by some waking-life person,
situation, personal impulse, or anxiety.

DREAM NOTES:

DATE:

DAY NOTES:

Do you dream of flying freely and joyfully?

You feel free to move through your outer life and inner space.

DREAM NOTES:

DATE:

DAY NOTES:

Do you dream of falling or drowning?

You feel helpless, insecure, or overwhelmed
about something in waking life.

DREAM NOTES:

DATE:

DAY NOTES:

Do you dream of discovering new rooms or neighborhoods?

You sense an opening up of new understanding or ability.

DREAM NOTES:

DATE:

DAY NOTES:

Do you dream of being lost or trapped?

You feel confused or uncertain about what
to do in some waking situation.

DREAM NOTES:

DATE:

DAY NOTES:

Do you dream of being well-dressed?

You feel good about your current appearance or life role.

DREAM NOTES:

DATE:

DAY NOTES:

Do you dream of being naked or wrongly dressed in public?

You feel vulnerable, overexposed, or out of place in some
waking situation, and feel ill-equipped to cope with it.

DREAM NOTES:

DATE:

DAY NOTES:

*Do you dream you are performing well in a test,
onstage, on the athletic field, or elsewhere?*

You are gaining assurance in your waking skills.

DREAM NOTES:

DATE:

DAY NOTES:

Do you dream about being injured or dying?

You feel emotionally hurt or nonfunctional about
something in waking life.

DREAM NOTES:

DATE:

DAY NOTES:

Do you dream of operating a car or other vehicle skillfully?

You sense a greater confidence in moving through life.

DREAM NOTES:

DATE:

DAY NOTES:

Do you dream you are in a natural or human-caused disaster?

You feel you're confronting a crisis in waking life.

DREAM NOTES:

DATE:

DAY NOTES:

Do you dream of rebuilding or constructing property,
or finding lost items?

You are healing from emotional or physical damage.

DREAM NOTES:

DATE:

DAY NOTES:

Do you dream you are having trouble with a car or some other vehicle?

You feel that things in your life are currently out
of control or otherwise unsatisfactory.

DREAM NOTES:

DATE:

DAY NOTES:

Do you dream that your computer, telephone,
or other machinery works incredibly well?

You feel that emotional and physical connections
are going smoothly.

DREAM NOTES:

DATE:

DAY NOTES:

Do you dream you are having trouble with a test?

You are confronting a waking-life challenge and fear failure.

DREAM NOTES:

DATE:

DAY NOTES:

Do you dream of traveling with ease to foreign lands?

You feel increasing ability to cope with life's problems.

DREAM NOTES:

DATE:

DAY NOTES:

Do you dream of missing a boat or some other vehicle?

You feel you've missed an opportunity in waking life.

DREAM NOTES:

DATE:

DAY NOTES:

Do you dream you are witnessing natural beauty or miracles,
or participating in sacred rituals?

You feel in touch with special levels of life.

DREAM NOTES:

DATE:

DAY NOTES:

Do you dream your house or other property is damaged or lost?

You feel emotional turmoil and/or physical damage.

DREAM NOTES:

DATE:

DAY NOTES:

Do you dream you are being healed, born, or reborn?

You sense a new beginning is near.

DREAM NOTES:

DATE:

DAY NOTES:

Do you dream you are menaced by someone who is dead?

You feel concern in waking life for the well-being of someone
who has died, or you feel guilty or afraid for yourself.

DREAM NOTES: